African Dwarf Frogs as Pets

The Ultimate Pet Guide for African Dwarf Frogs

African Dwarf Frogs General Info, Purchasing, Care, Cost, Keeping, Health, Supplies, Food, Breeding and More Included!

By Lolly Brown

Foreword

African Dwarf frogs are usually sold with other fresh or tropical water fishes. And because of their small size, they are sort of water species that can be kept in small vases or something of a living art. As a matter of fact, the African Dwarf frogs usually don't compete well with other freshwater fishes especially the aggressive ones. This is why they fail to thrive in tanks or in a community aquarium. Obviously, these frogs need a spacious environment than a vase filled with water. Their tanks need to be lined with gravel as well for them to thrive.

This book will guide you on how you to properly care for your pet African Dwarf Frog. You'll get to learn more about its biological information, habitat needs, health, and the proper diet to keep your pet healthy and happy! Always keep in mind that not all frogs turn into a prince but they can be kept as great pets!

Table of Contents

Introduction

African dwarf frogs are also referred to as dwarf clawed frogs. These frogs need to be housed in an aquatic tank, and potential owners like you should make sure that there is at least two gallons of water per one frog. The bottom part of their tank should be filled with gravel. The gravel should be large enough so that they won't mistake it as food. Water must be filtered as well. You can use an undergravel filter, a sponge filter, or a canister filter. Around 10 to 20% of water should also be filtered out, and you must replace it with de – chlorinated water at least once a week.

Shedded skins, frog feces and leftover food should also be removed. You can use a dip net to aid the water filter so that it won't be filled too much.

African Dwarf Frogs need to reside in a dimly lit area in their tank so that they're not exposed to too much light. Those one inch diameter PVC pipes could be used as a hide though it may not aesthetically blend in with the rest of your tank design. Alternatively, you may want to use stone caves, submerged logs as well as other hide decorations provided that they are aquarium – safe. The water temperature should be around 78 to 82 degrees Fahrenheit. Make sure that it won't go above 85 degrees or below 70 degrees.

You can also use live plants like Elodea, or other types that are used for freshwater tanks. These things could be nice add – ons but make sure that enough light enters the tanks as the plants will need it for their health and also for their 12 – hour photoperiod. Plants are needed inside the tank that is usually where your African Dwarf frog will rest.

They typically hang around the plants near the water surface.

It's also best to have a branch or rock that is near the water surface because your pet frog would certainly want to rest there as well. Here's the thing, frogs still need to gulp air from time to time so that they can breathe. The shallow spots on the tank will allow your pet to breathe without needing to swim and struggle above the water surface.

African dwarf frogs can be fed with commercial pellets that are made for clawed frog species. You can also offer them sinking pellets that are designed for carnivorous tropical fishes. However, keep in mind that these commercial pellets should not be the only diet of your pet frog. Your pet will need other diet portions like thawed worms. You need to provide them with (frozen) black worms, white worms, brine shrimp and bloodworms. Make sure to rinse the shrimp well with clean water before feeding.

Your African Dwarf frog should eat at least thrice a week or more depending on its age and appetite. Make sure to remove leftover food after a few minutes to keep the tank clean.

When it comes to the lifespan, African dwarf frogs can live around 2 to 5 years or even longer as long as you provide them with the right care. Make sure to not release these frogs if you can't take care of them anymore. This is because they may carry diseases that can harm native frogs and other aquatic species. If you have unwanted frogs, you need to dispose it properly by finding a shelter through a local herpetological society. You can also ask if a pet store is willing to take your African dwarf frog.

In the next few chapters, you'll learn more about what African Dwarf frogs are and how you can provide them with everything they need. Read on!

Chapter One: African Dwarf Frog Facts

If you wish to add something new and also special to your fish tank, you might want to consider African Dwarf Frogs! African Dwarf Frogs are tiny tranquil frogs that are best for a small fish tank. As nighttime pets, you will only find them during the moonlit hours where you can witness some very witty things from them. Here's the catch though, your frog will not turn into a royal prince if you try to kiss it. Sorry! In this chapter, you'll learn the biological features of African Dwarfs as well as what you need to know to successfully keep them.

Biological Information

All of these frog species have quite a similar appearance. This is why they are often mistaken for one another. They don't have that distinct look on them. The main difference is where these frog species came from. African Dwarf Frogs is under the family of Pipidae, and genus Hymenochirus. There are four species that has the common name of African Dwarf Frog. These are the following:

- *Hymenochirus boettgeri*
- *Hymenochirus boulengeri*
- *Hymenochirus curtipes*
- *Hymenochirus feae*

For instance, the *Hymenochirus boettgeri* species is native to Central African Republic including other countries like Nigeria, Congo, Cameroon, Equatorial Guinea and Gabon. The *Hymenochirus boulengeri* species is native in the country of Congo specifically in the North – Eastern region. *Hymenochirus curtipes* is endemic in the Congo Republic, while *Hymenochirus feae* is native in the country of Gabon.

The African Dwarfs are completely aquatic frogs that are small in size. The maximum size of these frogs can only reach around three inches. In fact, these frogs only weigh a couple of ounces.

It is very often that this species are mistaken for the African Clawed Frog. This is because they look so alike and don't have that distinguishing features. Perhaps the slight difference is that, the clawed frog species are a bit bigger and much more aggressive.

Always remember that when it comes to purchasing your first frog, it's very important that you do your homework. You need to know the kind of species you want to buy based on the physical features that you have researched, and not just depend on what the breeder tells you or the label of the frog because sometimes it could be wrong.

African dwarf frogs have an average lifespan of 5 years. If you take care of it well, it will definitely extend their lives so make sure that you follow the guidelines later in this book.

African Dwarf Frogs Temperament

African Dwarf Frogs will make great additions to your aquatic tank, or aquatic collection. These frogs are nocturnal creatures. This means that they become active at night. As a completely aquatic creature, you can expect them to swim like fishes and spend most of their time under the surface. However, since they are amphibians, you can expect your pet frog to occasionally rise to the water's surface to inhale some air.

Keep in mind that these frogs can't spend a lot of time out of the water otherwise they will get dehydrated and can definitely die after 20 to 30 minutes. This is something that you should also remember whenever you're transferring your pet to another container whenever you're spot – cleaning its tank.

This is because unlike fishes, they don't have gills but they do have fully developed lungs. You can find them swimming quickly to the water's surface and gasp for air, then dive right back to the water. Another cool thing you need to know about these frogs is that they are known for doing a zen position. You might see your pet just floating to the water's surface without moving, as if they're dead but they're not! They are probably doing a meditation! You might see their arms and legs stretched out but don't fret because this is completely normal (for them!).

You might also hear your pet frog singing (a quiet buzzing sound) especially if they are ready to mate. This is usually how the male attract the female.

Appearance

African Dwarf Frogs are olive in color although there are frogs that have a more brown or greenish shade. This species vary quite in color but they have black spots on their bodies. As mentioned earlier, they are small in size and don't weigh much. They grow no more than three inches.

The species under the *Pipidae* family have no tongues and no teeth. These are some of their physical features. Their feet are webbed because it helps them swim fast, and also enables them to feed themselves. They also possess a buccal cavity. It enables them to draw in water and also allows them to eat by sucking the prey into their mouth.

Another distinct feature of African Dwarf frogs is that they don't have ears. They become aware of surroundings through the special sensory lateral lines on their body which functions as their sensory to detect vibrations and movement.

Males and females African Dwarf frogs also differ a bit. Females are quite larger and have a more prominent genital area which is called ovipositor. On the other hand, male African dwarfs have a tiny gland at the back of their front limbs. The function of this gland is not yet known but it's believed that they use it whenever they are mating.

Chapter Two: African Dwarf Frogs as Pets

Having a pet is a lasting commitment, and also having stated that, you need to truly be literally, financially, and also emotionally all set in order for you to maintain your pet delighted, satisfied, as well as safe. You have to likewise get expertise on exactly how such animal behave prior to you bringing them in your home. You must ensure that both your individuality and also your family pet will certainly jive. Through this chapter, you will have an overview on just how African Dwarf Frog behaves as family pets. Their personality will be discussed for you to examine whether you can get along with them or otherwise. Factors regarding frog licensing in addition to the papers you required to prepare will also be discussed in later sections.

Do You Need Permission to Keep African Dwarf Frogs?

If you're thinking about purchasing a African Dwarf Frog, you must be knowledgeable not just on their attributes yet also to the particular regulations or constraints that you need to observe in order to keep them legitimately. Like in any kind of animal licensing, the constraints in addition to the requirements will certainly differ depending upon the nation, area, or state that you belong. It will be better if you speak with any type of lawful authorities near your location. Likewise, you can do your very own study in your area or online.

The Convention on International Trade in Endangered Species (CITES) for wild fauna and plants is the one in charge of looking after plants as well as animals of various types particularly the ones who are taken into consideration as threatened. This organization is quite vocal to their campaigning for against over- exploitation of animals and also plants through international trade. Roughly 30,000 types of plants and 5,800 varieties of animals are being secured by CITES. Majority of the nations belonging in the significant continents in the globe like

Europe, USA, Latin America, Australia, as well as Asia have come to be a part of the organization.

CITES Appendices

Convention on International Trade in Endangered Species for wild animals as well as flora has three appendices. In each appendix is a listing of various plant and also animal varieties classified in different ways when it comes to its rules in exporting, keeping, as well as trading.

Appendix I is composed of types that are taken into consideration as most jeopardized among any various other animals and plants provided by CITES. These types are threatened with extinction. Appendix II is a checklist of species that are not necessarily endangered with termination currently however the chance of it depends on just how carefully controlled the animal trade is. Appendix III is composed of types with varieties asked for by various organizations that manage animal trade in the varieties resulting to the need for teamwork from various other countries in order to protect against unlawful or unsustainable exploitation.

Frog Licensing

It is recommended for you to have your frog accredited to save you in case of any type of difficulty. Sometimes there are veterinarians who examine the certificate of the pet frog in order for them to make certain that you are keeping your animal legitimately. If you wish to travel and planning to bring your frog with you, having it licensed will certainly be a fantastic help given that other countries, as well as even airline companies, are requiring pet licensing before taking a trip.

Generally, you do not need to have approval from wild animal organizations or authorities in order to have your frog licensing. All you have to do is to offer a record with the name, identity of the species on which your frog belongs. There is a demand for you to offer details like name, address, call information, and the signature of the previous owner or on where you bought your frog is additionally needed. You additionally have to provide your personal info and also other needed information. This type of paper needs to be maintained for future recommendation for you as the brand - new owner of the frog until it is offered or if it dies.

In the United States, there is no government legislation that mandatorily requires licensing for pets, wild or exotic animals, and amphibians. Nonetheless, this is being selected in the state level. As a result, it is suggested that you examine the regulations being prevailing in your town, district, or state. You might ask the authorities in your location to ensure that you are having the ability to abide by what is required. Ensure that you'll have the ability to follow with the guidelines and also laws in your location to stay clear of issues in the future.

Frog Maintenance

Having family pets, as a whole, can be pricey no matter if it's a low upkeep or a high maintenance one. Either of the two, you need to provide for them sufficiently as it is crucial for them to stay in a healthy way of life. Though frogs appear like little creatures that are easy to take care of and also to keep, the truth is that cost can also add up especially on the initial phase. It is required for you to give everything that your frog needs in order for it to live satisfied as well as pleased.

Though it looks straightforward, these little pets will definitely add up on your everyday budget plan. The whole price of these frogs - related costs will certainly differ relying on where you acquire the materials, the brand name it belongs, the number of nutrients existing, the time being, and so on.

If you intend to seriously own a African Dwarf Frog as a pet you ought to have the ability to cover the required expenses it involves. The initial expenses connected with maintaining African Dwarf Frog consist of the cost of the species itself. In addition that you will need to pay for its substrate, habitat equipment, preliminary medical check - ups, licensing, food, and also various other accessories needed.

Cage or aquatic tank, food, and water equipment, medical care, cage decoration or accessories, products for breeding, treatment, as well as the cost of a African Dwarf Frog itself are the general cost for maintaining such species. It is highly advised for you to buy only from reliable and also official frog breeders to make certain that the frog you purchased is healthy and balanced and also as much as possible is a captive - bred. You might purchase from online pet stores or sites as well as on amphibian's conventions. It is best to request references to make sure that you will be able to handle a well - regarded breeder alone.

Costs

The cost of an African Dwarf frog varies. Its price actually depends on its age, color, availability and the breed or species it belongs to. If you want to purchase a frog with a lower cost you may transact with backyard breeder but at your own risk since if you're going to acquire frogs from them, you wouldn't be so sure that the frogs are well-taken care of or if they are really a captive - bred or have just been randomly captured in the wild. Remember not to purchase a cheap frog if it is in the expense of its health and quality. African dwarf frogs, on average, cost $1.50 to $5. Usually, the younger ones are being sold at a lower cost than the adults.

A frog needs its own place to stay in order to feel relaxed, safe, and comfortable. It is ideal for you to mimic its natural habitat for it to be able to adjust easily on its new surroundings. In buying an aquatic tank, make sure that it is appropriate for the size and age of your frog. The enclosure should be made out of glass so that you can easily monitor your pet, regulate temperature, and for the reason that this kind of tank will be easier to clean. You may buy an enclosure along with a screen lid for as low as $20 but it greatly varies depending on the size, brand, and quality of the cage. The cost of it can further increase up to $50.

Temperature and humidity inside the cage should be properly maintained. Therefore, tank heater along with thermometer and hygrometer will be needed. In order to simulate a healthy environment for your pet, you should be able to set up its tank as if it's living in the wild. You may add cage decors such as branches, leaves, live plants, moss and other things that would make the cage pleasing to the eyes. It is up to you what supplies or accessories to use. Just make sure that you will not overdo it. Tank accessories might cost you around $15 or more.

It is not really that necessary for African dwarf frogs to have access on UVB Lighting but having one won't hurt. If ever you will add a plant inside the cage, the UVB lighting will be a great factor for it not to wither.

Chapter Three: Where to Buy African Dwarf Frogs

After understanding all the lawful needs in addition to the temperament of this amphibian, it's now time for you to be able to know where and also to whom you can acquire a healthy breed of African Dwarf Frog. This part can be really critical as this the moment in which you're most likely to choose the pet you're going to invest the rest of your time with. In this chapter, we'll help you know whether the breeder you are handling is respectable or not.

Plus, we'll offer you ideas on where you can buy an African Dwarf Frog. You will be guided on how to determine a healthy frog from an undesirable one.

Sources of African Dwarf Frogs

There are lots of frog breeders marketing African Dwarf Frog. Getting from them might look appealing as they truly understand just how to persuade consumers. However, you have to take safety measures as well as hesitate prior to getting it. You cannot be specific on the health and wellness of the frogs in their protection. There's a chance that these frogs are unlawfully imported from the wild and that they probably endured from poor health problems arising from importation damages. Frogs who have actually resided in the wild may deal with problems when they have actually been caught. It might face problem in adjusting to its new atmosphere. Make certain that the backyard breeder you are negotiating with has a great reputation.

You may look at the closest pet store shop in your location if they are offering African Dwarf Frog. Make certain that the store has provided an excellent living condition for the frog. Don't hesitate to leave if you found otherwise. If the frog has actually been maintained in a not so good setting there's an opportunity that it carries specific diseases. It is not suggested for you to buy in pet shops considering that it is believed by some animal organizations that their market is made to make profit out of the cost of these wild animals.

You can also go to amphibian conventions, which is exclusively made for hobbyists. In here you can meet reputable sellers and other frog owners as well. You can get referrals from other patrons in order for you to now to whom should you purchase a frog. This is not a daily event. You have to wait for months or years before another convention will be held in your place. Make sure to always ask for referrals before dealing with breeders. There are several forums online on which they are giving reviews and recommendations of several breeders.

Captive – Bred African Dwarf Frogs

It is suggested for you to obtain a captive - bred frog. This type of frog might be a little pricey however it will certainly be much more cost-effective in the future. If you buy a captive bred frog, you can be sure that they have actually been taken care of correctly. There is no opportunity that they are bringing any kind of illnesses which can help you save from medical costs. They can conveniently adjust to the new environment they belong to compared to those that have actually been captured in the wild.

Quarantine Tips

There's a possibility that the frog you have actually bought is lugging illness that might not be harmful to them but might possibly impact you and your various other pets as well. It is the main factor why have to have your frog under quarantine for a couple of days. This procedure may not be necessary if you really trust the breeder but you still have to deal with it otherwise; it is an excellent way for you to guarantee the wellness and safety of everyone in your home.

There are whole lots of aspect that might influence the health of your frog. Stress from shipment and also taking a trip can trigger a covert condition they bring. The food that they ate before being caught is an element also if ever before they have been captured from the wild.

Quarantining your African Dwarf Frog is done in order to diagnose if your pet is dealing with infection in addition to analyze the health problem of your pet. It is the way to guarantee that the frog you have actually acquired is not carrying any infectious diseases. From this, you can prevent any type of health issues to be moved to the entire family.

In order for you to have effective quarantine duration for your African Dwarf Frog, initially you need to offer a correctly sanitized quarantine storage tank. A 10 to 20 gallon tank can be used. Make certain that your frog has accessibility to water in any way times. Screen the moisture and also maintain the sanitation inside the cage. After establishing up the container, place your frog inside it. See to it that your hands are clean prior to and after managing them. Allow your frog remain inside the quarantine container for around more than a month. You might bring an example of your animal frog's fecal example to your veterinarian and also have it examined.

African Dwarf Frog Breeder

Locating a well - regarded breeder can be a little bit challenging and yet it is extremely essential. It is important as they mirror the kind of upbringing the frog had. If the breeder is responsible as well as caring, you can be sure that the frogs they have reproduced were elevated in a healthy atmosphere. Here are the following steps for you to be able to choose a reputable African Dwarf Frog breeder:

Time to investigate! Doing a history check is the preliminary action. Make sure if the breeder has a site because this is where you will get information and also verify it. Make sure to check the material of the site. The contact information should be there as well. In addition to that, the facilities of the breeder should ideally be shown. Look for licenses, registrations, and other records confirming that they are marketing frogs legally. If the website of the breeder seems suspicious or not well - attended, then just leave the site and find a legit breeder.

Make sure to contact the breeder and as much as possible meet him/ her. You may request their experience when it comes to looking after a African Dwarf Frog and also just how long they have actually been breeding African Dwarf Frog. It's also ideal if the breeder have some sort of health warranties. You can ask information concerning the frog's registration and wellness details. One great indicator that the breeder you are having a conversation with a reputable frog breeder is when he/she inquire about you also. A good pet breeder would make sure that the frog he bred will go to the right owner.

You may also want to request for an ocular visit so you can check inside the facilities of the breeder. If he permits you to do so, it means that they are not hiding anything and that the breeder is caring properly for the African Dwarf Frog. Inspect the location where the frogs have been raised. Observe the surroundings and also make certain that it is tidy and enjoyable. If the environment seems unclean as well as unorganized, do not deal the breeder.

Selecting an African Dwarf Frog

After you find out exactly how to determine a trustworthy breeder, the next step is for you to know what signs to try to find in order to pick a healthy African Dwarf Frog. The skin needs to be intense and also clean. It should not have scratches, swellings, dry skin, as well as inflammations. The eyes must be clean and also devoid of any type of haziness or cloudiness as these may show an illness. The frog must be active. Indications of being bloated, inactive, and also lazy should not be present. The frog should look passionate. It must be able to consume correctly during feeding time.

Health Concerns of African Dwarf Frogs

Most frogs tend to be generally healthy and long-lived. However, there might be tell-tale signs. You need to evaluate the living conditions such as wrong temperature, high levels of ammonia, finding traces of water, fouled soil, and excessive light. This could contribute to depressed immune system and illness.

Signs of illness include if your frog might have unusual behavior. There is a gradual or sudden weight loss.

You can see weight loss around the abdominal area, which starts to look hollow, and you may even see the outline the backbones and hipbones. There is an excessive digestive gas that is associated with overeating, intestinal parasites, oversized prey, intestinal infection, gas bubble disease, or even respiratory infection. There might be red blotches that are caused by hemorrhaging, or white blotched that is caused by fungi. You can see that there is a fuzziness or cloudiness in the frog's eyes. There is a general swelling in the frog's head, body, or even the limb. This could be the result of poor water quality to bacterial infection, kidney diseases that would cause edema. Your pet could spend too much time in hiding.

It is drinking or eating less, and there is a tremendous weight loss. However, before you judge that your frog is not eating, you need to give a variety of food before you judge that it is sick. If you think that it is truly sick, bring a stool sample to your vet. If it does not have any stool, you need to bring in a whole frog. You can see discolored skin; the joints are swollen. There is a great discharge from the nose, eyes, or mouth. You can see runny droppings that would occur for more than two days. If you see that frogs are yawning too much, this could be a symptom of a disease with no cure.

You can prevent this and give your pet a good health and long life through designing and maintaining a tank, you should also manage its temperature, water quality, light, furnishing, topography, and diet needs of your frog. You need to constantly check these conditions because this plays a critical role in preventing the onset of diseases.

Here are some other health issues that could arise if you buy from illegal breeders or if you don't quarantine your pet frog:

Bacterial Infection

Your pet frog is regularly exposed to bacteria, but sometimes, the bacteria are fought off by their mighty immune system. If your pet is stressed out paired with an depressed immune system, the bacteria can fully invade. Some stressful conditions are foul water, overcrowding, and improper temperature. You need o make sure that you can provide proper husbandry to lessen the risk of your frog's stress.

Loss of appetite, listlessness, redness on the underside of the thighs and belly, excessive skin slough, skin shedding, loss of appetite are some signs of bacterial infection. If you do not notice this infection, there could be more extreme neurological signs. Bring your frog to the vet immediately; s/he will prescribe tretracycline bath and antibiotics. These baths may become stressful and could be very ineffective.

Fungal Infection

The fungal infection could infect scrapes or wounds, which is very common for tadpoles. This infection could be easily treated topically by removing your pet from the water and daubing mercurochrom, malachite green, or hydrogen peroxide.

Herpes Virus, Iridovirus and Ranavirus

Your pet frog is very susceptible to various viral diseases. The most common virus that your pet easily contract is the herpes virus. The herpes virus causes kidney tumors. This would affect the kidney, which will cause hydrops and hydrocoelom. Your animal would easily lose weight and would die after spawning. Another virus is the Iridoviruses, specifically the ranaviruses, is the subject for many years. These viruses are responsible for eradication certain breeds of frogs.

Generally, amphibian viruses are very uncommon to general population. However, more of them are slowly being discovered because of the increased interest in the disease in both wild and captive frogs

How to Prevent the Spread of Salmonella

Salmonella microorganisms are quickly spread from amphibians to human beings. Human beings might come to be contaminated when they touch something that has actually been in contact with the feces of amphibians, and after that put their hands in their mouths. As an example, babies have become contaminated after consuming from bottles of infant formula that came to be polluted throughout the preparation.

People that prepared the formula had actually not washed their hands after touching an amphibian or because such animals were enabled to walk near where the food is being prepared.

For Salmonella bacteria to spread out from animals to humans, the bacteria need to be ingested. As a result, simply touching or holding a frog will not result in spread of microorganisms unless something infected with amphibian feces or the frog itself is put in the mouth.

The majority of Salmonella infections in humans result in a light, self-limiting ailment identified by diarrhea, fever, and stomach cramps. However, the infection can spread out to the bloodstream, bone marrow or nerves, causing extreme and also occasionally deadly, ailment. Such severe infections are more probable to occur in infants as well as in people whose body immune system is endangered (as an example, bone marrow transplant recipients, persons with diabetes mellitus, individuals infected with the human immunodeficiency infection, and also radiation treatment patients).

However, Salmonella microorganisms cannot be gotten rid of from the digestive system of amphibians. The administration of prescription antibiotics to eliminate these bacteria has actually been not successful and may cause the appearance of Salmonella germs that are immune to prescription antibiotics. Try to elevate or recognize amphibians that do not lug Salmonella bacteria have actually been not successful; as a result, microbial society of feces examples in an attempt to determine amphibians that are not lugging Salmonella bacteria is not advised.

The good news is, the spread of Salmonella germs from amphibians to people can be quickly prevented by using implementing the following safety measures:

- Constantly wash your hands with warm, soapy water after taking care of amphibians, cages and equipment, and also the stool of your frog.

- Do not permit your pet to have access to the places where food is prepared. Additionally, do not enable amphibians to have access to washroom sinks as well as bathtubs or to any kind of location where babies are bathed. Think about keeping your amphibians caged or limiting the parts of your home where amphibians are enabled to roam around. Constantly wash your hands after entering into call with any type of area where amphibians are enabled to stroll complimentary.

- Don't eat, consume, or smoke while taking care of your frog, cages, or devices. Do not kiss your pet frog or share food or drink with them.

- Do not utilize the kitchen area sink, kitchen area counters, shower room sinks or bathtubs to bathe reptiles or to clean amphibian cages, dishes or fish tanks. You may wish to purchase a plastic container or bathtub in which to shower or swim your pet. Drainage and also fecal material should be thrown away properly instead of the bath tub or house sink.

- The Centers for Illness Control and also Prevention suggests that kids much less than 5 years old should stay clear of contact with frogs or other amphibians. Homes with children less than one year old shouldn't ideally own amphibians. The Organization of Reptilian and also Amphibian Vets urges amphibian hobbyists with children to discuss steps to reduce threats related to owning these pets with their veterinarian as well as their physician.

- Youngsters should be overseen when they are taking care of animals to make certain that they do not put their hands or objects on the frog and right into their mouths. Amphibians must also not be maintained in childcare centers.

- Immuno - compromised individuals ought to avoid contact with amphibians.

- Make sure to comply with instructions from your frog's vet. You must take note of providing the correct diet regimen and environment for your amphibian. Healthy and balanced amphibians residing in correct environments are less prone to breeding of Salmonella bacteria.

It's not indicated to inhibit frog ownership. With a couple of exceptions (as an example, babies or immune - compromised individuals), many people have a reduced threat of obtaining salmonellosis from frogs, but this risk can be minimized even further by adhering to basic safety measures. Amphibians like frogs can be safely kept as family pets; however hobbyists like yourself ought to recognize the approaches for lowering their danger of acquiring Salmonella bacteria from your pet amphibians.

Chapter Four: Habitat Requirements

As you now know, African Dwarf frogs came from Africa and they can be found in the freshwaters of Gabon, Cameroon, Congo and Nigeria. They are endemic in rivers near tropical forests as well. The environment in the African continent is warm and humid which is why light is very important for your pet from even if they are nocturnal creatures. They still need around 10 to 12 hours of light cycle and darkness inside their tank. African dwarf frogs need a humid environment and clean water in order to survive. Just like other aquatic pets, it's best to set – up a tank and create the right setting before you even buy one.

Tank and Set Up

You need to ensure that the temperature above the water surface has a very high humidity level – in this way when your pet frog goes above the surface, they won't easily get dehydrated. As mentioned earlier, light is essential. You need to simulate the environment they have in the wild. Make sure to set up your light on a timer as they need to have regular periods of dark and light (10 to 12 hour cycle). You don't need to provide them with fancy lighting like other common amphibian or reptile pets, a normal LED aquarium light will do.

Another important factor to keep in mind is that their skin is very sensitive. This is why you need to provide with good filter as well as a test kit because you need to make sure that the water has a great quality and doesn't contain chemicals. You need to always check on the water and ensure that you do a 20% weekly water change.

The temperature should ideally be around 72 to 78 °F. The pH level should be 6.5 to 7.8; gH should be 5 to 20 and kH should be 4 to 15.

For the substrate, you can choose gravel or sand. If you purchase gravel then make sure that the grains are large enough so that your pet won't be able to swallow them or confuse them as food. You shouldn't also have a strong water movement. Your pet won't like strong current because they like to be motionless in the water. They like it calm and peaceful. Remember the zen position they often do?

Even though frog species can breathe it's best that you consider purchasing an air stone or pump in order to keep the optimal quality of water as well as keep the bad anaerobic bacteria away from your set – up.

Keep in mind though that they are also sensitive to vibrations and loud noise. You must isolate the pump from the tank glass in order to avoid this. You can also add a layer of insulation like a piece of cloth or styrofoam between the stand and the tank. Your pet African Dwarf frog also loves a live plant. You can buy Hornwort, Java Fern or other rooted type of plants. Just make sure that you cover the plant roots so that your frog won't dig them out.

You also need to provide lots of hide caves around the tank because in the wild they are naturally being preyed on since they are small creatures. Your pet will feel safer if there are hiding spaces in the tank. You can do this by purchasing hiding spaces from pet stores, using plants, or driftwoods.

Aquatic Tank Size

Most aquatic pet owners start with a 10 gallon tank that is large enough to house around five frogs. However, bigger is always better! It is best that you use a 20 gallon tank for your pet, though make sure that the water isn't too deep so that your African dwarf can easily go to the water surface for air.

Tank Mates

African Dwarf frogs can live with Neon Tetra. They are the perfect pair of species for tropical freshwater tanks. Just make sure that you keep them well – fed and that the water conditions are set up correctly to avoid any problems.

These frogs are peaceful creatures which is why it should be placed with similar creatures.

Other ideal tank mates include small fishes such as the following:

- Guppies
- Platies
- Mollies
- Danios
- Corydoras
- Rummy Nose Tetra
- Serpae Tetra
- Bamboo Shrimp
- Cherry Shrimp
- Ghost Shrimp
- Some snail species

However, you have to be careful if you are going to put shrimps and snails in the tank because your pet frog might consider them as food. A good rule of thumb is that the tank mates shouldn't fit inside the mouth of your African Dwarf.

Don't house them with aggressive fishes like Cichlids because they will stress out your pet and might also prey on them.

You can also keep them with a Betta but proceed with caution. This is because there are some betas that are aggressive though there are also some that don't bother other tank mates. It all comes down to the Betta's individual temperament. Obviously, if the Betta is aggressive, it will stress out your pet frog and can even kill it. So just keep an eye out to see if they will be compatible with one another. Generally speaking, African dwarf frogs are quite social creatures and can live with other peaceful sea creatures of at least 2 per tank.

Tank Options

Before you even buy your African Dwarf Frog, you need to make sure that you have already set - up the house a week in advance. This move will ensure that you to check all the components of the frog house you are working on. There are many kinds of aquatic tank that you can purchase, but more on that later.

The size of the cage should be around 10 to 20 gallon, This would provide enough room for your frog to maneuver around the terrarium. There are various types of aquatic tanks you can buy which are also applicable to other frog species if you are also planning to own a couple of collections in the future. It includes terrestrial tank, aquatic tank, half and half tank, and arboreal tank.

Terrestrial tank are suited for frogs who prefer drier climate. This will just consist of a substrate and a water supply that could either be a water bowl or a small pool. House frogs do not really like this environment in the long run. An aquatic tank is just the same set - up as for fish, or in short, an aquarium with water – this is what your African Dwarf Frog needs.

Another type is called the half and half tank. This is the most common set - up that you can also do. This will consist of half water and half land aquarium set-up. You can do this in a lot of ways; you can fill the tank with water and then put in large rocks to become land-masses. You can also buy special separators to divide water and land masses. And last but not the least is an arboreal tank. This tank is for frogs who like to stay up high on tree branches. Essentially, you will purchase a tall tank and put small trees beside it.

Substrate Options

Substrate is the soil, sand or bedding material that you put at the bottom of the tank. The basic function of the substrate or the bedding is to absorb the waste that your African Dwarf Frog created. However, there are also other purposes of the substrate like maintaining the level of humidity inside the terrarium; it could also retain moisture inside. It offers a cushion against a glass bottom or a hard plastic, provides a shelter for burrowing and it could be a great source of heat for your pet.

Different reptiles or amphibians need different kind of substrate. You also need to consider your African Dwarf Frog's feeding needs. Substrate components could be ingested and could cause blockages and impaction, so make sure to use the right kind of substrate. In some occasions, you can mix and match different kinds of substrate. You need to also plan on how to clean your pet's cage.

In some cases, you do not really need any substrate in your frog's aquarium. You can put a drain at the bottom so you can easily hose down the aquarium. However, you may need to frequently clean the substrate as it may become unaesthetic ally pleasing.

You can use a layer of newspaper and/or paper towels if you are okay with the regular clean-up. However, some may need to be changed more than once a day in some situation. Some reptiles need paper towels as their substrate. For amphibians, you need to use plain paper towels because those with colors could be harmful. Aside from this, you need to closely pay attention on the wetness or dryness of the paper towels. Wet paper towels are breeding grounds for unwanted bacteria. Other than that, reptiles and amphibians can't really burrow under paper towels.

You can also provide mats, carpeting, and liners. This is another simple substrate option that you use for your amphibian or reptile. These things are just like your paper towels and magazines; however, you do not need to throw this out immediately. However, you may need to purchase two sets of mats, when one will be soiled, you can replace one while you wash the other one and dry it out.
This requires frequent cleaning and not suitable for pets that needs moisture in their terrarium.

Another kind is the small animal bedding. This kind of substrate is usually used by hamsters, guinea pigs, and other small pets. This is made of bedding and shavings made from recycled paper products. However, this is not really appropriate for amphibians because it spoils when it becomes wet.

Then there's moss. You can easily find moss at garden centers and pet stores. Some of these things are ornamental, which means it should not be used as a substrate, but decors or accents in the terrarium. There are other mosses that are suitable to be substrates for reptiles, but not suitable for amphibians. These are the typical green mosses that you can see in pet stores that are put in bales or bricks. This kind of moss does not really hold moisture.

The sphagnum moss can be tan, pink, or brown in color. This grows in bogs and will decay in soil additive. This kind of moss can be used alone for many amphibians and lizards. You need to place this correctly under shelters and substrates. This kind of moss is actually acidic, so it is not a good option for burrowing and terrestrial amphibians.

Another type is soil blends. There are soil mixtures easily available at your nearby pet stores. There are available soil substrates that you can use to make your own ingredients. Different soils have different characteristics. It is quite difficult to evaluate their suitability as a substrate. Do not use soils that have rocks, or vermiculite. You should only use soil blends that are sold from pet suppliers from direct pet suppliers.

Soil actually works well for burrowing and terrestrial species that comes from tropical or humid environment. You still need to pay attention to the moisture content of the soil. You still need to have a drainage layer of gravel or other material so the soil does not become waterlogged. If the soil becomes too wet it will spoil and some types could possibly irritate the skin. Some amphibians could possibly ingest this soil.

Another type is the coconut husk fiber. Some of these things are sold in dry compressed brick. This is made from ground up fibers of coconut. When you place this in water, this expands and becomes excellent substrates for both amphibians and reptiles. If you are able to maintain its cleanliness, you do not replace this often. This kind of substrate holds moisture well. You can mix this with other kinds of substrate blend to make your own substrate for your pet. However, this could cause irritation for amphibians if it has not expanded and settled down well before use. It would even spoil if it comes in contact with water for long periods of time.

Alternatively, you can use coconut husk chunks. These chunks are also available for dry compact brick. This consists of hairy coconut fibers around the coconut shell that did not fall on the ground yet. These things have similarities with coconut husk fiber, but these are larger and may be prone to be a problem if ingested by your pet. Often, this substrate is mixed with the fiber or sol. When mixed with other stuff, it really improves the drainage in a tropical terrarium.

Leaf litter is actually collected rather than purchased in places. Leaf litter can form a bulk of your substrate that is suited for some reptiles and amphibians. This works well if mixed with soil, coconut fiber, and some other natural substrate. Magnolia and live oak are the common barks used. You can either used this alone; however there is a potential risk of infectious diseases or pests especially with freshly collected leaves. To prevent this, you need to wash the leaves under hot water and then have it air dry in the sun for several days. You can also microwave the leaves to kill pests.

Previously, this is the only natural substrate for amphibians and reptiles. This fir bark is natural and can potentially retain humidity in an enclosure. However, this is not appropriate for all species. The main issue for this type of substrate is that your pet could ingest while eating.

Cypress Mulch is another substrate for amphibians and reptiles that are made from wood. This is widely available at garden centers and pet stores. This Cypress Mulch can work very well in humid or moist conditions than other substrate. You can use this for both amphibians and reptiles.

Unfortunately, this kind of substrate is not really sourced in a sustainable manner. The logging of these things damages both the wetlands and important habitat.

Commonly Used Materials for African Dwarf Frogs

Play Sand or Calcium Sand

This kind of substrate can be used alone for some amphibians. Some owners use this alone, but you need to check it for rocks or debris that will cause problems when your pet ingests this. There are sands that are made from calcium carbonate, which are much safer to use because it will be less likely to have an issue with impaction.

Gravel and Stones

Many kinds of rocks, gravel, and stones are available for your pets. However, you need to be careful when using this kind of rocks as substrate. If your pet has ingested this, it will be very difficult to pass through the body. In order to avoid the blockages, you need to use stones that are too large for your pet to swallow. Aside from this, you also need to avoid aquarium gravel; you can use this if you put it under another substrate as a drainage layer.

Housing Tadpoles

If you plan to have your own tadpoles, make sure you have a good sized container for your tadpole, such as a swimming pool, aquarium, garden pond, or even a plastic container. You need to keep them outside that would mimic their natural environment and give them enough sunlight; however, you need to keep the container partially shaded.

Tadpoles like to have shallow water. You can place smooth gravel or rocks at the bottom of the pool. When you see that they are already maturing, they would want to get out of the water, you can place a partially submerged rock, piece of wood, or gravel that would lead to the land. You need to have a place where you can put your frogspawn. You need to put weeds if you do not have stones or rocks. Putting weeds would oxygenate the water which would help the tadpole to grow. The weed would have algae and bacteria on them; this will serve as your pet's main food source until they can hunt on their own.

Tadpole Pond

If you ever plan to create a tadpole pond, you only need to give de - chlorinated fresh water. You can remove chlorine for the tap water by letting it sit for around 24 hours before you put it to the pool, or, you can treat the water with de - chlorination drops that are meant for aquariums.

Tadpoles are very sensitive to chlorine and heavy metal. In small spaces, the water needs to be frequently changed to maintain great quality. Scoop around a third of the water and replace with clean and de - chlorinated water. However, you need to remember that these tadpoles should not be handled during the water change because their skins are very sensitive to the natural oils, soaps, and chemicals that are found in our hands. Rinse your hand before and after tank maintenance, feeding, or any other task relating to your pet.

Feeding Tadpoles

Your tadpoles diet depend on the species, but most of the tadpoles are herbivores. You can give them thawed or frozen leafy lettuce such as spinach or romaine. You can also boil them, but boiling means a loss of nutrients, and when frozen, it is very soft enough to be eaten. You can also give a good quality of flake fish food and crush algae tablets, which you can find at aquarium shops, at extreme cases, you can even find tadpole food at pond shops. Only feed small amounts a couple of times a day. If you feed them excessively, it will create water - quality problems. Use a small fish net to scoop out any uneaten food.

Habitat Health Issues

Here are some health issues that could arise if you don't set – up a clean environment for your pet:

Frog Parasites

Amphibians are also prone to various parasites. This includes protozoa, trematodes, nematodes, and cestodes.

Entamoeba ranarum and Amoebiasis are very common and can be treated easily if you catch this early. Roundworms, also called the nematodes, are the most common parasites seen in amphibians. Lungworm, also known the rhabdias, could be easily found in small numbers. This is contagious to other amphibians, so, if you have an affected animal, you must quarantine it and keep it separated until you have properly treated it.

Frog Bloat

Impaction depends where you house your frog. Your frog could ingest some of substrate when they are trying to grab a prey. Some small gravel could be easily passed through the feces, but larger gravel could remain in the intestinal tract that could cause the blockage.

To prevent this impaction, you can provide alternate substrate to your pet frog. If you see that your frog is impacted, you may feel your frog's belly, and if there is a hard lump, there is probably a substrate that your frog could not digest. In rare cases, your frog might excrete the substrate slowly throughout a period of weeks. If the condition continues to persist, consult the vet immediately to have it removed.

Chapter Five: Food Guidelines

African dwarf frogs eat both meat and plant – based foods. However, they are more of a meat eater or a carnivore. Make sure to provide a variety of meal to make sure that your pet will receive all the nutrients for them to stay healthy. There are lots of pre – prepared foods that are available today in the market which should compose the base of their diet. Most of it are usually pellet – based.

You can also provide your pet with various treats once or twice a week. These may include brine shrimps, mosquito larvae, earthworms, bloodworms, fish fry, and krill.

You can also feed them with beef heart but just do this once a month since it's very fatty. At the end of the day, it's down to your own preference and also to what your pet likes. You can opt to feed them with live or frozen food as well.

While they are tadpoles, make sure to feed them once a day but as they grow older, feed them less. As an adult, you can just feed them once every 2 days. Make sure to offer bite – size foods and remove any leftovers after a 20 to 30 minutes.

It's also important to not overfeed them because if you do it would most likely lead to obesity and also poor water quality. All of these can contribute to various health issues for your pet.

If your pet seem to lose its appetite or are being fussy, you might want to use tongs so you can feed them directly. It's best that you place their food directly where they can see it to encourage eating.

Health Issues Related to Food

Here are some health issues that could arise if you don't provide the right nutrition for your pet frog:

MBD

This is a common disease among the captive amphibian, such as the African Dwarf Frog. This would cause deformities and soft bones in the skeletal system. If you are not giving your frog food that is enriched with calcium or calcium + D3, your frog would develop metabolic bone disease.

The signs of this disease are failure to grab prey, droopy lower jaw, muscle twitching, backbone and pelvic deformities, and listlessness. You can treat this disease through consistently coating the food with calcium and vitamin D. However, if your frog is having a hard time grabbing the prey, because the bones are too soft, you would need to administer the calcium + D3 with a syringe through the frog's mouth once every one to two days until the frog's bones start to harden.

Amphibian Hypovitaminosis A

This is a common result of low vitamin A in the frog diet, or also known as the short tongue syndrome. Squamos Metaplasia is a condition that is a result of low vitamin A level. Your pet will have an inability to produce proper sticky mucus that is needed on its tongue. You can easily see this when your toad or frog tries to grasp the prey properly, and it does not stick easily to the tongue when it is retracted into its mouth, and its prey easily goes away.

Aside from the aforementioned signs, hypovitaminosis A could easily affect the conjunctiva around the frog's eyes (just like swelling) as well as the kidney and bladder infection that would lead to hydrocoelom. The treatment of this disease will involve life threatening conditions and supplementing vitamin A in the diet, as well as correcting the frog's diet and any other underlying cause.

Endoparasites

Tapeworms, roundworms, and pinworms are very common among toads and frogs. Some of these endoparasites are not really that harmful for your frog, but if you see a parasite, immediately consult your vet. S/he will diagnose the parasites and treat it before it gets too late. Parasites are easily transferable, so make sure you quarantine new amphibians before you introduce new pets to your old pets.

Amphibian Corneal Lipidosis

Some characteristics of this disease include whitish plaques, deposition of cholesterol deposit in the cornea. The cause of this disease includes high cholesterol level which is result of diet high in fat. There is no strict treatment for this, but you may correct the diet to prevent the condition to further worsen.

Gout

This condition is the deposition of uric acid crystal in different location in your pet's body. The cause of this problem includes diet that is very high in purine, infection, dehydration, and kidney failure.

The crystal will slowly form in soft tissues such as the kidney and liver, but could form larger stones that you can find in the bladder. If your vet already diagnosed this, it is actually sever now. These bladder stones can be easily removed by your vet.

Chapter Six: African Dwarf Frog Evolution

African Dwarf frogs go through collection of stages before they reach their adult years. They start to exist as a teeny small egg and ultimately turn into these exotic and also yet attractive vibrant species. It is very fantastic how life functions. How a single egg can develop into an animal such as this. For you to know better about this frog, we'll give you a glimpse on the phases it deals with prior to it reaching adulthood.

You'll be able to discover what occurs as each phase passes and you'll understand just how transformations actually function. This is going to be an interesting journey so buckle up as we offer you the life cycle of African Dwarf Frog.

Reproduction Process

African Dwarf frogs are taken into consideration polygynandrous when it involves mating like many anurans. In some breeding programs for captive - bred, males are usually found to be calling as well as attracting female frogs under simulated hefty rainstorms just like what they do in the wild. Having the ability to reproduce, the setting they got used to will certainly help them adjust and also do the process of reproduction easily.

Research studies reveal that hefty rain occasions are what cause the frogs to mate. Therefore, this condition ought to be taken into consideration if you are going to breed your African Dwarf Frog. After calling out for companions and discovering a match, the male will cling to the female or will go through the so - called amplexing. Afterwards you might expect 8,000 eggs per clutch. Eggs that have been fertilized will certainly be deposited on stationary water or in little ponds. It might occupy to 36 hrs prior to these eggs hatch out.

Frogspawn

The eggs are enclosed in a jelly - like substance which safeguards them up until they hatch. It is usually sticky and it also enters into a black as well as white color. They will certainly drop directly to stagnant water or small ponds particularly on the surface area of the water. Each egg comes in the size not bigger than two millimeters. After three days, these eggs will transform right into tiny tadpoles. The more eggs the frog lays, the more possibilities that some of them will certainly endure.

When frog eggs clump with each other as they stream in the water they are called frogspawn. For a fact, larvae are able to spot or pick up neighboring killers through vibration and also to conserve themselves from being consumed, the eggs will certainly hatch out earlier than the usual time for hatching. This process on where embryos or eggs hatch out early in order to protect themselves is called phenotypic plasticity.

Larvae Phase

Tadpoles are just a half centimeter in length making them a welcome prey for pets larger than them. They appear like so much of a fish's physique as they additionally utilize their tails for swimming and their gills for breathing. This phase will typically last for 2 to 3 months. They prey on tiny bits of nutrients located in water through the usage of filtration.

As they grow, they will certainly establish small legs that will assist them emerge from water and also crawl towards the land. Its tail will eventually diminish as apoptosis occurs on which the cells die which leads to the re-absorption of the body components or body organs.

Their lungs will certainly likewise start to create as their gills disappear. Their eyes will certainly likewise be rearranged as well as the development of eyelids will certainly be present. Their skin will end up being tougher and thicker. Body parts such as its tongue and jaw will certainly begin to form.

After the tadpole has completed the procedure of apoptosis, it can currently end up being terrestrial and relocate right into places in the fashion of powerful jumping with the usage of the suction cups discovered on their toes. Generally they hide under the plants or burrow themselves under mud.

Froglets Phase

African Dwarf Frog can actually be a fantastic family pet for new keepers and even for people that does not have any experience on dealing with frogs. They are generally calm and very easy going. Before taking into final thought whether or not this type could be right for you and your household, you have to initially make on your own accustomed to this frog breed.

Adult Frogs

It takes almost a year before a frog totally matures but in the case of a female African Dwarf frog, it takes a bit of time before it becomes a fully - grown adult, when this happen you can easily see the difference through its color and size. Females grow larger than male. Their color ranges from green and greyish shades. They will stay on rainforests, vegetation, or even on highly distributed urban areas. After they have become mature frogs, the process of reproduction may now occur and the cycle will go back to the first stage.

The Goal of Breeding

Breeding your frogs can be an exciting event in your life. You can watch these translucent eggs develop into tadpoles. You need to be ready for the intense work you will do if you would want to raise your own frog colony. You will spend a lot of money than you might think. As we have said earlier, monetary gain should never be your first goal in this endeavor. In most cases, first time breeders may barely break even. You will need to purchase or provide several things such as rain - chambers, nursery tanks, filters, water conditioners, lighting, filters, heating, tiny insects, morph tanks, and other necessary things.

You need to spend an extensive amount of cash from the beginning. The goal of breeding should only be the love of the breed and the love for knowledge and the excitement of this specific endeavor. Some breeders may only do it with the sole intention of saving the specific species. The ecosystem that you will provide needs to mimic their natural environment. This would give them the advantage to grow up and bring it closer to being a full grown frog. Other things that it must mimic are the rain, stress, vitamin and food sources, humidity, and warmth. You need to control the ecosystem cycling, or controlling these external factors.

A misting routine is a system that is very critical for breeding your frog. It could be very complicated to set up on timers, but very simple if you just spray on tanks. In some cases, you need to supply the tank with heavy rains in a rain

- chamber (or a breeding chamber); if you are very serious about breeding your frogs, you would develop this chamber.

Breeding Chambers

If you plan on becoming an avid frog breeder, you need to have rain - chamber. This is a necessary tool that would help start the breeding cycle in the colony. If you already have an aquarium for your frog, you need to use a separate tank for your rain - chamber. The main purpose of this chamber is to stimulate seasonal or monsoonal rains of the frog's homeland, and this will indulge them to reproduce. The large amount of water in this chamber will create this effect.

If you only use your typical aquarium, your set-up would be destroyed by floods and dislodging plants, this might also cause fungal infections in your frogs. Even though your frogs are naturally aquatic, setting up a rain - chamber is a great idea. You would take out the egg masses out of the main tank and make them into adults, it would be easier for you to remove and fully take care of them. In order to prepare for this event, you need to spray mist the aquariums and increase its amounts daily. However, do not over mist to the point that you can smell rotting plant materials, where your plants and soils are soaked so much that it will die. This misting activity will start the male to croak. This would develop their nuptial pads in front of the hands. Males may even become too territorial.

When you are ready to introduce the frogs into the tank, you may need to have a boom box placed near it, playing rain forest sounds or even their species' croaking sounds and other environmental background music. This will help the frogs go into breeding mood. You can also look for tranquility music; however, make sure that there is no symphony music behind the rain forest sound. Make sure that you loop the sound that you will be using.

Breeding Chamber Introductions

The best time to introduce the frog into their rain chamber is when the males are already calling nightly and they already have their nuptial pads ready, and the females are already ripe with their eggs. You can let the frogs stay for around a week, but not over two weeks. Make sure that both of the frogs are fed well before the breeding process, you can also add calcium supplement to the prey that they will be eating. Add enough water into the chamber and allow it to "rain" for around three to six hours a day. Continue this process until the frogs have already laid enough eggs.

If your female frog has already laid more than enough. Over - breeding is very unhealthy for our female frog, this would deplete them with nutrients, proteins, and enzymes in their bodies which they need to continue to grow. Your females may continue to lay eggs without the hay, but it would not be fertile. Do not allow the male and female to fertilize the egg more than you can take care of. If you can see that they have done the task, remove them immediately and sterilize again.

Frog Gender

Before anything else, the very first step you need to do in regards to breeding your African Dwarf Frog is to be able to identify the sex of frogs. Unlike various other animals, the sex-related dimorphism of frogs can be very hard to establish given that the majority of frogs have their genital areas internally. It can be a bit tough but if you will really look, you'll have the ability to do a successful frog sexing.

You might do this by observing the physical attributes of your frog. Females show up larger as well as possess a more brilliant color than males. An additional method to figure out whether your frog is a male or female is through the sound it makes. Usually, male frogs develop a specific sound when they are finding for a companion throughout the reproduction period. Via "calling", they can draw in females who are prepared to breed. If you find it difficult to establish the sex of your frog, you may seek aid from your vet.

Breeding Fundamentals

When it comes to breeding your African Dwarf Frog there are some actions that you need to take. First you have to establish the appropriate environment for your frog. You need to be able to imitate its all -natural environment throughout the breeding season. Generally, frogs breed throughout the wet season. Most scientists agree that hefty rains are what trigger most frog species to reproduce including the African Dwarf Frog.

Make sure you'll give the appropriate setting for your frog through establishing the correct environment with using manipulating its cage. You may cut down misting and also reduced the temperature of your frog's cage for about 5 levels Fahrenheit. After a month, you can return the typical level of its temperature. You can greatly haze the tank and make sure to give lots of food. By doing this you are able to simulate seasonal changes to your animal.

Prior to the breeding period, your African Dwarf Frog will undergo the procedure of estivation or hibernation. Usually, they burrow themselves under mud or moss and they might likewise hide behind plants. You might start to decrease moisture level and also temperature when you have actually observed that your pet frog has been staying under its substrate longer that it normally does. When your frog is prepared, it will certainly go out from its hiding area and for a couple of days it will consume a whole lot. After that, it will certainly await breeding.

Male frogs would certainly do some specific sounds in order to call out for its mate. If it has actually already discovered one, you can expect the breeding process to start. See to it to provide plants in order to make sure that your female frogs will be able to place its eggs inside the tank.

Spawning

The term spawning is the term use for hatching in frogs. Expect that a female African Dwarf Frog can produce

8,000 eggs per clutch. When it has actually laid the eggs, make sure to divide it from its mother as it has the tendency to eat its offspring. Each egg comes in the size not larger than two millimeters. It might take 3 days prior to the eggs hatching out. By that period, you have to provide extra water inside the cage.

Tadpole Upkeep and Metamorphosis

Caring for tadpoles can actually be a challenge so you should be very certain that you are prepared to reproduce your frog. After the hatching of eggs, tadpoles will certainly emerge. The stage of being a tadpole generally last for 3 to 4 months. They eat tiny bits of nutrients located in water through making use of purification. As a whole, they are cannibals therefore it is advised that you will place them into separate jars as they have the tendency to eat each other once they are positioned on the exact same enclosure. Make certain to clean up the containers prior to placing them in it.

You might also supply a separate cage loaded with live plants. There is a tendency that you might shed a number of tadpoles yet still, this can be easier for you particularly when you are concerning to feed them. You may spray finely - ground fish food for your tadpoles. Make certain that you will be able to maintain the high quality of the water inside the tank by changing it occasionally through the usage of an aerator to avoid old food from remaining in it.

As tadpoles grow, they will certainly begin to deal with adjustments in regards to their body framework. The duration of apoptosis will certainly take location or the process on which cells pass away and trigger the re - absorption of the body organs or body components of the tadpoles that are thought about repetitive. Their gills will eventually vanish as their lungs develop. They will have thicker as well as tougher skin. Its tail will go away as their legs establish, and more changes in its appearance will change. After this tadpole metamorphosis phase, they next stage is adolescent frog or infant frogs. You may feed young ones with wingless fruit flies and small crickets. Make sure that you will give the correct husbandry to these young frogs.

The Right Breeding Practices

In order to end up being a reputable frog breeder, you must devote your effort and time. If ever before the reproduction wasn't successful, it's okay! Accept the truth that not all frog breeding leads to a success in creating eggs. See to it you will be able to supply all the important things required by your pet from the setting down to the specific care it calls for. Ensure that you will be hands - on during the period of reproduction. For a bigger chance of an effective reproduction, it will be much better for you to have a higher proportion of frog instead than having one set. This is because having competitors can very well encourage reproduction. A bigger number of male compared to females can cause the male frogs to become much more energetic for breeding purposes.

These are just some important guidelines that you need to know about breeding and the general life cycle of your frog. If you are really serious in breeding them, make sure you have enough time and money to do this task, remember, you should not do this for the money. Aside from this, you need to have access to regular information and even a healthy support group that would help you during this endeavor. You need to have someone by your side to help you with the tasks.

First Few Days

Your African Dwarf frog can be quite fuzzy especially during the very first week of its stay. With proper socializing, your pet frog will surely get use to you as its brand - new owner but it will happen gradually. Don't expect for your new pet to easily get accommodate. Give it time to adjust to its new surrounding and as you do this, make sure that your frog's needs are met. Through this chapter we'll provide you pointers on exactly how you will appropriately manage your African Dwarf frog. You will also learn additional guidelines on how you can care for this creature.

Keeper's Secrets

It is essential for you to know how you can deal with your pet frog. By doing this, you'll be able to see if your characteristics match well with an African Dwarf Frog. It's best that you know how they are in terms of temperament so that you'll know what to expect. Here's the thing, keeping an African Dwarf Frog is not easy and also takes passion. Even if amphibians in general are low – maintenance, they will still need your time and attention.

Unlike common household pets, African Dwarf frogs just like other frog species do not enjoy being handled as much as possible. It is advisable for you to manage your pet frog just when it is needed. One example is if you need to spot - clean its tank. Prevent unnecessary handling because way too much of it might trigger tension to your pet frog. When you are managing your frog, you may utilize protective gloves. The residue from your hand may really infect your frog and the toxin it produces can create allergic reaction or irritability to your skin. Consequently, it will be better if will use gloves in order to prevent transfer of illnesses, and also protect your frog from acquiring one.

When they feel intimidated, your pet might produce a white liquid material. This is their protection mechanism against potential threats. The fluid can actually cause skin irritation or allergic reaction to human beings. Sometimes, they try to jump when they feel like they need to safeguard themselves. As stated earlier, stay clear of unnecessary handling to avoid yourself from causing stress and anxiety to your pet.

African Dwarf frogs are not really aggressive but they can be if it's feeding time or whenever they pick up danger in the surroundings. However, you don't need to work about it because African Dwarf Frogs won't bite you since they don't have a teeth.

Skin Sloughing

There may be some circumstances that you will discover little bits of skin inside your frog's cage. Do not fret since it is a natural condition that amphibians lose skin. If you see indications of skin shedding, you can try to haze your pet in order to make the shedding full. When it has already removed, expect that your African Dwarf frog will certainly eat it later on.

Estivation

African Dwarf frogs estivate during the completely dry period. Estivation is the term used to coin hibernation period. It is the process in which the frog form a cocoon of skin and mucous. It will certainly burrow itself in mud or hide under plants. When the stormy season comes, it will certainly come out from estivation and would eat for a couple of days. From after that, it will certainly continue straight to reproducing fish ponds and companion.

Spot - Cleaning

Unlike other family pets, they ought to not be cleaned up with using bathing items as they can be potentially hurt or eliminated by these chemicals. Although they require no pet grooming, it is still necessary for you to maintain the cleanliness of your frog as well as its health with effectively cleaning and also disinfecting its enclosure or tank.

If you're planning to keep froglets at home or you want to become sort of a backyard breeder, it's now time for you to discover the essentials of breeding a frog. Who knows? You might end up being one of the most well - regarded frog breeders in your neighborhood! This component will actually be valuable as you'll be given with topics like how to identify your frog's gender or sex dimorphism as well as how you can establish the right breeding practices.

Chapter Seven: Husbandry for African Dwarf Frogs

You may need to clean the aquarium just the same way as you do for other aquatic pets you may have. However, you need to do it routinely as your frog will shed more often. If you plan to have a half and half set-up, figure out how to get a filter that would work, but not affect the land substrate. You can have under gravel filter, just the same as the over - the side filters. Although frogs are pretty low-maintenance pets, you still need to provide them with clean environment to keep them healthy.

These little creatures shed regularly, secrete mucus through their skin, bathe in their water bowls, eat live animals, which would contribute greatly on the waste built - up in their tank.

You need to clean the entire frog aquarium regularly, as well as to change the water to prevent both bacterial and fungal infection. It would be tiresome experience at first, but it would not really take much time soon enough. You just need chlorine treatment tablets, paper towels, colander, scrub brush and temporary housing.

Spot – Cleaning Tips

Prepare the water ahead. Make sure you already have chlorine - free water that you would use on your tank. You need to leave the water sitting overnight. Remove the frog and place them in a temporary place, just like in a jar, if you plan to do a complete and thorough cleaning. If you do not want to prepare a jar, you can buy a small plastic tank with the sole purpose for cleaning. These tanks are easily available in most pet stores. However, if you are just tidying up and changing the water, you can leave the frog sitting in the frog.

Make sure Remove 25% to 75% of water from your frog's tank. The percentage of water would easily depend on how dirty the water is and how long you have made a partial water change. You may use a siphon hose, filter, or a plastic container to remove the water. You need to also remove most of the substrate or gravel from the bottom of your tank, especially if you are doing a thorough cleaning and sanitizing to treat some common disease. If you are just spot cleaning, it is key to leave some substrate and gravel behind. Put your substrate on a fine colander, then use a hot water and scrub brush to clean away the debris or any algae present. Rinse well and have it air dry for some time.

Inspect if there are any pieces of food hidden inside your frog's aquarium or any uneaten insects on it. Remove anything that you can find. If you leave things on the tank, this would promote bacteria and fungi growth that would seriously affect your pet's health. Also see the skin shedding of your pet, you can inspect it and see if your frog is healthy. Remove all the plastic plants and decorative items. Make sure you scrub them thoroughly and rinse well and return these things to the tank.

Wipe the outside and inside of the aquarium with toilet papers. Remember; do not clean the tank walls with any chemical cleaners as they are very harmful to your pets. Replace the substrate or gravel carefully and slowly. Put new water to the frog aquarium to carefully replace the water you have removed. If your frogs are purely aquatic, refill the tank. If they are just terrestrial, replace the water from the frog's swimming area. Return your frog. Give them enough time to adjust to the new and clean environment before you disturb them again.

How to Remove Waste in the Tank

Removing tank waste is a frequent upkeep that you need to do in your frog's aquatic tank. Uneaten and left over insects could seriously create a lot of wastes. These dead insects would create molds and would become a source of unwanted waste. Remove these things as soon as possible. Rotting and fallen plants are another form of waste that is often overlooked. If you see a plant that is starting to rot or die, you need to have it removed immediately. A large dying plant in your frog's tank could create too much waste that the aquarium could handle. However, fallen leaves that are left to decompose on their own usually do not present a grave problem. Other common wastes include skin shedding, infertile eggs, animal feces.

A tank that you have set-up for a few months, it should have a lot of beneficial bacteria that would help take care of the waste. In addition, there are a lot of microorganism and small helpful invertebrates you can introduce in a terrarium. You can do this by mixing leaf compost from outside into the substrate or soil.

Do's and Don'ts

In some cases, you may come across problems concerning the husbandry that you have set-up for your pet. You might have overlooked some things because it might look teeny tiny to you. Your frog is relying on water for its life. A small alteration in the water quality could lead up to significant diseases, and could sometimes, lead to death.

If you believe your frog is sick and planning to take it to the vet, make sure to bring a sample of the water as well. However, do not bring your pet in the water, instead, put the water in another container and bring it to you for the frog's exam, so the water could be tested for quality issues.

Your vet will evaluate dissolved oxygen, pH, chlorine, pathogens (bacteria), nitrate or nitrite, ammonia, and harness. In these parameters, if some of it out of range, it will be easily corrected. Problems concerning chlorine and ammonia could be easily treated with sodium thio - sulfate baths or fresh water baths. The nitrite and nitrate issues may respond to methylene blue baths.

Many amphibians need an aquatic environment. Aside from that, the need a specific humidity in the enclosure or they might suffer chronic dehydration or even worse, desiccation. Some amphibians can handle a certain degree of dehydration, in some cases; some can even handle 30% without suffering from extreme damages.

Unfortunately, some animals do not respond positively to dehydration, some may even succumb to kidney damages after a few days to a few weeks. Some symptoms of dehydration are sunken eyes in their sockets, dry to tacky skin, color changes, and a thick slim coat. Your frog will have a decreased activity as well as its food intake. You can easily correct this problem by placing the amphibian in chlorine - free, well - oxygenated water at its preferred and well-maintained body temperature. In rare cases, you may need to give them supplemental fluid. Immediately bring your frog to your vet to administer replacement fluid intracoelomically in certain situations.

Abrasions and Injuries

Most of amphibian's skin is delicate. A slight human touch could cause their skin extreme damage. Transport bags or even abrasive nets could harm the slime layer and the skin. If you need to handle your frog, you need to wear wet latex gloves that are cleaned thoroughly with chlorine free water before you touch your African Dwarf Frog.

Cage furniture, plants, rocks, and substrate could cause abrasion to their rostrum, feet, skin, and belly. Once the skin is damaged, the risk for infection increases dramatically. Bite wounds, rubbing nose on the glass or skins, fighting, and any other physical barrier could be a source of potential infection. You need to cover your glass covering with paint, change your metal screen to soft nylon, and separate animals from sizes, especially the aggressive ones. You need to ask your vet how to give first aid on these injuries or even systemic antibiotics and pain medications as your frog needs it.

Hypothermia vs. Hyperthermia

Hypothermia is not really that life threatening if you caught this early. The frog could be slowly re - warmed to its proper temperature. If you have exposed it to cool temperatures for long periods of time, immune - suppression is possible, as well as deleterious effects on the pet's gastrointestinal tract.

If your frog has recently eaten and then exposed to extreme temperature that would be too cool for digestion, intestinal upset and vomiting could result. Aside from this, hyperthermia is not really lethal if you catch it early. Some signs of hyperthermia include uncoordinated limbs, hyperactivity, lethargy, and ultimately, death. Just like hypothermia, your pet should be placed in fresh, chlorine-free water at its proper temperature to increase the body temperature. If your animal have been severely heat stressed, it may need vet intervention to have fluids and corticosteriods injected.

Toxicities

Your pet frog is extremely sensitive to its environmental toxins, due to their permeable skin and their high surface area to body weight ration. Iodine, quanternary ammonium, ammonia, chlorihexidine, and chlorine are some disinfectants that are highly toxic to your amphibian. Many of these things could be easily absorbed in plastic containers and would possibly leech out. So even though you do not see the disinfectant, you need to use a glass or stainless steel for your pet frog.

Reddening of skin, increase mucus production in its skin, blood spots on the skin, difficulty in breathing, hyperactivity to lethargy, convulsions, tremors, paralysis, vomiting, diarrhea, and death are some signs of toxicity. However, the toxins and its signs vary greatly in species. Cigarette smoke and pesticides are shown to be toxic to amphibians. You need to keep your pet in a smoke free environment.

These are the essential things that you need to purchase and do to have a conducive and healthy environment for your African Dwarf Frog. Keep in mind to purchase these things before you bring your frog at home. If you will not provide these things, you may compromise your frog's environment and its health.

Chytrid Fungus

This occurs for lowland and upland stream frogs. This disease was discovered in 1999 but could be responsible for the decline of the frog population in the 1970. There are spores of fungus that grows of the outer layers of the frog's skin; this would then result to keratin damage that would kill your frog in 10 to 18 days. The spores of this fungus can be transported via wet soil or water.

Toxic Syndrome

You need to ensure that your frog's water is changed frequently because your pet absorbs water through their skin. If you ever leave foul water in the substrate, some toxins could be absorbed through your pet's skin – which will eventually lead to a disorder. Spastic extension of hind limbs, cloudy eyes, erratic jumping, and listlessness are some of the symptoms of the toxic - out syndrome.

You can easily treat this disease by placing your frog in a shallow water dish of clean water then you leave your frog there. You need to replace the water every four hours or until the signs of the syndrome goes away. You also need to closely monitor the outside conditions so you can protect your pet frog from having this toxic out syndrome.

Water Edema Syndrome

In this syndrome, your frog will start to swell up because of too much water retention. In very rare cases, your pet frog may feel like a water bag. Some common causes of this disease are a damaged lymph heart and kidney disease. Unfortunately, there is no known information as to how to prevent this disorder. You may limit the amount of water available to the frog, or your trusty vet could release retained water through small incisions at specific swell sites, but this will be a very tedious process.

Fungal Infection

One of the most common fungi among the amphibians is the Batrachochytrium Dendrobatidis, which is the agent of chytridiomycosis. Although most of the fungal infections are seen in immunocompromised amphibians, B. dendrobatidis could cause disease in healthy frogs.

Signs of this B. dendrobatidis could vary from sudden death to no sign to slowly onset, starting with the reddening of the belly (which is similary for dermatosepticemia), excessive skin shedding, and lethargy. If you catch this early, treatment could be very effective.

There are also other fungal organisms that could cause disease in amphibians. Saprolegniasis would produce cotton - like growth on the mouth and skin of your pet frog. Chromomycosis, a pigmented fungus, could be seen in various amphibians. It would produce light - tan to dark - gray nodules on the skin. If you do not treat this, this would result to death. Most of these fungal diseases are the result of underlying poor environmental condition and stress. You need to correct these deficiencies because this is mandatory to have a successful treatment and prevention for other future diseases.

Cancer Tumors

Cancer tumors can also affect your pet frog. Some common form of cancers is of the kidney, gonads, liver, and skin. One of the main symptoms is hydrocoelom.

Blindness

Your frog's blindness is primarily caused by lipids on the corneas. Aside from this, there is also a high fat diet because you may have fed too much meat in its diet. At this moment, there is no cure for this disease, but you can prevent this disorder by feeding your frog a low - fat diet.

Conclusion

African dwarf frogs are delicate and sensitive animals. As an amphibian, your pet might also be a danger to you. They're not venomous but most amphibians including frogs may carry Salmonella bacteria, which is usually on their feces or on their skins.

Salmonella is the most common form of bacteria that amphibians carry and something that can be transferred to humans. This is why it's highly recommended that you do not touch your frog as much as possible. If for some reason you need to handle your pet, like if you need to transfer them temporarily on another tank, make sure to thoroughly wash your hands after touching them, or better use gloves instead.

Since these African dwarf frogs are sensitive, make sure to avoid placing sharp materials inside the tank. You need to also make sure to check the gravel or the tank décor you're going to use in order to also keep your frog safe from hazards or possible injuries.

One of the most common health issues of African dwarf frogs is called dropsy. This condition is fatal for pet frogs. If your pet acquires this disease, the frog will start becoming bloated and it will also start to show distress. This type of disease is caused by various bacterial and parasitic infections.

Dropsy can be treated depending on the cause though it's also contagious. If your pet has dropsy, it's best to bring him or her to the vet who specializes in amphibians. Other health issues are fungal infections which appear as fuzzy patches on the skin of the frog. There's also another fungus known as Chytridiomycosis and if your pet is infected by this, you need to isolate him to keep your other collections safe.

Glossary of Frog Terms

Advertisement Call - Males frogs 'and toads ' mating call

Aggressive Call- Territorial Call; it is a call made by male when another male comes too close

Amphibian- double life; animals that are vertebrates and lives a part of their lives in water

Amplexus- A position wherein the male frog is on the top of a female in order to externally fertilize the eggs

Anura- tail-less; the order of toads and frogs

Archaeobatrachia- ancient frogs

Army- a collective term used to define a group of frogs

Aquatic- lives in water

Bask- to sit under the sunlight in order to warm up

Beaufort Wind Scale- a kind of scale used to monitor and estimate the speed of the wind

Binomial Nomenclature- biological name assigned to every living thing

Boss- an area on the toad's head between the eyes that is raised

Carnivore- species that eat meat

Chorus- a large group of singing, calling toads and/or frogs

Chytridiomycosis (BD) - Chytrid; a fungus of frogs that affects their skin's permeability

CITES- The Convention on International Train Endangered Species of wild fauna and flora

Citizen Scientists- citizens who contribute scientific information for various researches and projects worldwide

Cold-blooded- Ectothermic

Detritus- decaying animal matter and plant settling at the bottom of the pond

Digits- toes or fingers

Distress call- a call made by a frog or toad in order to discourage a predator

Dorsal- upper side

Dorsolateral- stripes or parallel folds along the back of a frog

Ecosystem- the interaction between the environment and living organisms

Ectothermic- the ability of a specie to control its body temperature through the use of available surroundings

Genera- related species that share the same first name

Habitat- it is where plant, animals, and other species live and grow

Herbivore- a specie that feeds on plant

Herpetologist- a scientist who studies amphibians and reptiles

Herpetology- The study of Amphibians and Reptiles

Insectivore- a specie that feeds on insect

Invasive Species- species that are not native to an area and cause ecological harm

Invertebrate- a specie without a backbone

Knot- a group of toads

Lateral- side surface

Mesobatrachia- Middle Frogs

Metamorphosis- stages of change that a specie undergo

Nictating Membrane- inner eyelid which is transparent

Paratoid glands- toxin glands found behind the eyes of toads

Phenology- Study of the Seasonal Timing of Events

Polyplois- having one or more than one sets of chromosomes

Pollywog- tadpole

Pupil- part of the eye on which the light enters

Ranavirus- a kind of disease of amphibians

Release call- a call made by a female when she's not yet ready or a call made by a male if another male thought he's a female

Spawn- eggs of frogs and toads

Submerged- beneath the surface

Tadpole- a frog's larval stage

Taxonomy- classifying all living things based on their similarities and differences

Territorial Call- Aggressive Call

Tibial gland- a gland found on the lower leg

Toe Pads- sticky area on the toes

Tubercle- Rough area on a toad's body

Tympanum- eardrum

Ventral- refers to the lower surface of the body or belly

Vernal Pools- Temporary ponds that are filled with water seasonally as the snow melts or when it rains

Vocal sac- an expandable sac found beneath the frog/toad's throat

Wetland- wet area between deep water and uplands

Photo Credits

Page 1 Photo by user stevengosch via Flickr.com,

https://www.flickr.com/photos/steveng4444/7625010292/

Page 5 Photo by user patterned via Flickr.com,

https://www.flickr.com/photos/patterned/3330232148/

Page 11 Photo by user Matt Reinbold via Flickr.com,

https://www.flickr.com/photos/furryscalyman/342233857/

Page 19 Photo by user leenient via Flickr.com,

https://www.flickr.com/photos/leena/290875417/

Page 36 Photo by user leenient via Flickr.com,

https://www.flickr.com/photos/leena/302431199/

Page 56 Photo by user leenient via Flickr.com,

https://www.flickr.com/photos/leena/302431247/

Page 62 Photo by user Jason Fether via Flickr.com,

https://www.flickr.com/photos/ourdreamsarethesame/37734
25397/

Page 83 Photo by user leenient via Flickr.com,

https://www.flickr.com/photos/leena/280445407/

References

A Set-up Guide for New African Dwarf Frog Parents - Petsmart.com

https://www.petsmart.com/learning-center/fish-care/a-set-up-guide-for-new-african-dwarf-frog-parents/A0090.html

African Dwarf Frog: hymenochirus curtipes – Petco.com

https://www.petco.com/content/petco/PetcoStore/en_US/pet-services/resource-center/caresheets/african-dwarf-frog.html

The Definitive Guide To Caring For African Dwarf Frogs – FishKeepingWorld.com

https://www.fishkeepingworld.com/african-dwarf-frog/

How to Keep and Care for African Dwarf Frogs – MyFroggycam.com

https://www.myfroggycam.com/

African Dwarf Frog Care Guide (Diet, Tank & Breeding) – FishKeepingAdvice.com

https://fishkeepingadvice.com/african-dwarf-frog-care/

Caring for African Dwarf Frogs - Aquariumcoop.com

https://www.aquariumcoop.com/blogs/aquarium/caring-african-dwarf-frogs

Basic Care: African Dwarf Frog – Azeah.com

https://azeah.com/frogs/basic-care-african-dwarf-frog

Caresheet: African dwarf frog - Aquariadise.com

https://www.aquariadise.com/caresheet-african-dwarf-frog-hymenochirus-genus/

African Dwarf Frog Care – PetHelpful.com

https://pethelpful.com/reptiles-amphibians/African-Dwarf-Frog-Care

A Care Sheet for an Underwater Dwarf Frog – Mom.me

https://animals.mom.me/care-sheet-underwater-dwarf-frog-4197.html

African Dwarf Frog - Frogpets.com

http://www.frogpets.com/african-dwarf-frog/

www.ingramcontent.com/pod-product-compliance
Lightning Source LLC
Chambersburg PA
CBHW062000040426
42447CB00010B/1840